50 Cooking with Miso Recipes

By: Kelly Johnson

Table of Contents

- Miso Soup
- Miso Glazed Eggplant
- Miso Ramen
- Miso Marinade for Fish
- Miso Roasted Brussels Sprouts
- Miso Caramel Sauce
- Miso Dressing for Salad
- Miso Butter Corn
- Miso Chicken Stir-Fry
- Miso Tofu Salad
- Miso Grilled Shrimp
- Miso Mashed Potatoes
- Miso Vegetable Curry
- Miso Honey Glazed Carrots
- Miso Pasta
- Miso Egg Salad
- Miso Barley Bowl
- Miso Black Bean Soup
- Miso Garlic Green Beans
- Miso Cauliflower Steaks
- Miso-Coconut Soup
- Miso Quinoa Salad
- Miso Glazed Salmon
- Miso Hummus
- Miso Potatoes Au Gratin
- Miso Cabbage Slaw
- Miso and Maple Roasted Squash
- Miso Flatbread
- Miso Risotto
- Miso Aioli
- Miso Stuffed Peppers
- Miso Spinach Sauté
- Miso Noodle Salad
- Miso Gravy
- Miso Eggplant Stir-Fry
- Miso and Lemon Grilled Chicken

- Miso Chilled Noodle Bowl
- Miso Braised Short Ribs
- Miso Potato Salad
- Miso Glazed Tofu
- Miso Dipping Sauce for Veggies
- Miso Chive Butter
- Miso Sweet Potato Soup
- Miso Potato Wedges
- Miso Vegetable Tempura
- Miso Peach Glaze
- Miso Stuffed Mushrooms
- Miso Roasted Chickpeas
- Miso Tomato Sauce
- Miso and Seaweed Salad

Miso Soup

Ingredients:

- 4 cups dashi (Japanese soup stock)
- 3 tbsp miso paste
- 1/2 cup tofu, cubed
- 1/4 cup green onions, sliced
- 1/2 cup seaweed (wakame)

Instructions:

1. In a pot, heat the dashi over medium heat until hot, but not boiling.
2. In a small bowl, dissolve the miso paste with a bit of warm dashi, then stir it back into the pot.
3. Add tofu and seaweed, simmer for a few minutes.
4. Serve hot, garnished with green onions.

Miso Glazed Eggplant

Ingredients:

- 2 medium eggplants, halved
- 3 tbsp miso paste
- 2 tbsp mirin
- 1 tbsp sugar
- 1 tbsp sesame oil
- Sesame seeds (for garnish)

Instructions:

1. Preheat the oven to 400°F (200°C).
2. In a bowl, mix miso paste, mirin, sugar, and sesame oil to create a glaze.
3. Brush the eggplant halves with the glaze and place them on a baking sheet.
4. Roast for 25-30 minutes until tender and caramelized, garnished with sesame seeds.

Miso Ramen

Ingredients:

- 4 cups vegetable or chicken broth
- 3 tbsp miso paste
- 2 servings ramen noodles
- 1 cup mushrooms, sliced
- 1 cup bok choy
- Soft-boiled eggs (for topping)
- Green onions (for garnish)

Instructions:

1. In a pot, heat the broth and whisk in the miso paste until dissolved.
2. Add mushrooms and bok choy, simmering until vegetables are tender.
3. Cook ramen noodles according to package instructions and drain.
4. Serve the noodles in bowls, ladle the miso broth over them, and top with soft-boiled eggs and green onions.

Miso Marinade for Fish

Ingredients:

- 1/4 cup miso paste
- 2 tbsp mirin
- 1 tbsp sugar
- 1 tbsp soy sauce
- 1 lb fish fillets (e.g., salmon, cod)

Instructions:

1. In a bowl, whisk together miso paste, mirin, sugar, and soy sauce.
2. Marinate the fish fillets in the mixture for at least 30 minutes (or overnight in the refrigerator).
3. Grill or bake the marinated fish until cooked through.

Miso Roasted Brussels Sprouts

Ingredients:

- 1 lb Brussels sprouts, halved
- 3 tbsp miso paste
- 2 tbsp olive oil
- 1 tbsp maple syrup
- Salt and pepper to taste

Instructions:

1. Preheat the oven to 425°F (220°C).
2. In a bowl, mix miso paste, olive oil, maple syrup, salt, and pepper to create a glaze.
3. Toss the Brussels sprouts in the glaze and spread them on a baking sheet.
4. Roast for 20-25 minutes until crispy and caramelized.

Miso Caramel Sauce

Ingredients:

- 1 cup sugar
- 1/4 cup water
- 1/2 cup heavy cream
- 2 tbsp miso paste
- 2 tbsp butter

Instructions:

1. In a saucepan, combine sugar and water over medium heat, stirring until dissolved.
2. Allow to cook without stirring until the mixture turns amber.
3. Remove from heat and carefully whisk in heavy cream, miso paste, and butter until smooth.
4. Let cool before serving.

Miso Dressing for Salad

Ingredients:

- 3 tbsp miso paste
- 2 tbsp rice vinegar
- 1 tbsp sesame oil
- 1 tbsp honey or maple syrup
- 1 tbsp water (to thin if needed)

Instructions:

1. In a bowl, whisk together miso paste, rice vinegar, sesame oil, and honey until smooth.
2. Add water to thin the dressing if desired.
3. Drizzle over salads before serving.

Miso Butter Corn

Ingredients:

- 4 ears of corn, husked
- 3 tbsp butter, softened
- 2 tbsp miso paste
- Fresh cilantro (for garnish)

Instructions:

1. Preheat the grill to medium heat.
2. In a bowl, mix butter and miso paste until well combined.
3. Spread the miso butter over the corn.
4. Grill the corn for 10-15 minutes, turning occasionally, until tender and slightly charred. Serve garnished with cilantro.

Miso Chicken Stir-Fry

Ingredients:

- 1 lb chicken breast, sliced
- 2 tbsp miso paste
- 2 tbsp soy sauce
- 1 tbsp sesame oil
- 2 cups mixed vegetables (bell peppers, broccoli, carrots)
- 2 cloves garlic, minced
- Cooked rice (for serving)

Instructions:

1. In a bowl, mix chicken with miso paste, soy sauce, and sesame oil.
2. Heat a skillet over medium-high heat and sauté garlic until fragrant.
3. Add chicken and cook until browned and cooked through.
4. Stir in mixed vegetables and cook until tender. Serve over rice.

Miso Tofu Salad

Ingredients:

- 14 oz firm tofu, cubed
- 3 tbsp miso paste
- 2 tbsp rice vinegar
- 1 tbsp sesame oil
- Mixed greens (for serving)
- Sliced cucumbers and carrots (for garnish)
- Sesame seeds (for garnish)

Instructions:

1. In a bowl, whisk together miso paste, rice vinegar, and sesame oil.
2. Toss cubed tofu in the dressing and let marinate for 15 minutes.
3. Serve the marinated tofu over mixed greens, garnished with cucumbers, carrots, and sesame seeds.

Miso Grilled Shrimp

Ingredients:

- 1 lb shrimp, peeled and deveined
- 3 tbsp miso paste
- 2 tbsp olive oil
- 1 tbsp honey
- 1 tbsp lime juice

Instructions:

1. In a bowl, mix miso paste, olive oil, honey, and lime juice to create a marinade.
2. Add shrimp and toss to coat. Marinate for 30 minutes.
3. Preheat the grill and cook shrimp for 2-3 minutes per side until cooked through.

Miso Mashed Potatoes

Ingredients:

- 2 lbs potatoes, peeled and cubed
- 1/4 cup milk
- 3 tbsp butter
- 2 tbsp miso paste
- Salt and pepper to taste

Instructions:

1. Boil potatoes in salted water until tender; drain.
2. In a bowl, combine milk, butter, and miso paste.
3. Mash potatoes and mix in the milk mixture until smooth. Season with salt and pepper.

Miso Vegetable Curry

Ingredients:

- 1 tbsp vegetable oil
- 1 onion, diced
- 2 cloves garlic, minced
- 1 tbsp ginger, minced
- 2 cups mixed vegetables (carrots, bell peppers, cauliflower)
- 1 can coconut milk
- 2 tbsp miso paste
- Cooked rice (for serving)

Instructions:

1. Heat oil in a pot; sauté onion, garlic, and ginger until fragrant.
2. Add mixed vegetables and cook for a few minutes.
3. Stir in coconut milk and miso paste, simmer until vegetables are tender. Serve over rice.

Miso Honey Glazed Carrots

Ingredients:

- 1 lb carrots, sliced
- 2 tbsp miso paste
- 2 tbsp honey
- 1 tbsp butter
- Salt and pepper to taste

Instructions:

1. In a pot, boil carrots until tender; drain.
2. In a skillet, melt butter and mix in miso paste and honey.
3. Add cooked carrots, tossing to coat. Season with salt and pepper.

Miso Pasta

Ingredients:

- 8 oz pasta (spaghetti or any preferred type)
- 3 tbsp miso paste
- 2 tbsp olive oil
- 1/2 cup pasta water
- 1 cup cherry tomatoes, halved
- Fresh basil (for garnish)

Instructions:

1. Cook pasta according to package instructions; reserve 1/2 cup pasta water.
2. In a skillet, heat olive oil and add miso paste, stirring until combined.
3. Toss in cooked pasta, cherry tomatoes, and reserved pasta water until well mixed. Serve garnished with fresh basil.

Miso Egg Salad

Ingredients:

- 6 hard-boiled eggs, chopped
- 3 tbsp miso paste
- 2 tbsp mayonnaise
- 1 tbsp Dijon mustard
- Salt and pepper to taste
- Lettuce leaves (for serving)

Instructions:

1. In a bowl, combine chopped eggs, miso paste, mayonnaise, and mustard.
2. Mix until well combined; season with salt and pepper.
3. Serve on lettuce leaves or as a sandwich filling.

Miso Barley Bowl

Ingredients:

- 1 cup barley
- 2 cups vegetable broth
- 2 tbsp miso paste
- 1 cup cooked vegetables (e.g., broccoli, carrots)
- 1/4 cup green onions, sliced
- Sesame seeds (for garnish)

Instructions:

1. In a pot, cook barley in vegetable broth according to package instructions.
2. Once cooked, stir in miso paste until dissolved.
3. Top with cooked vegetables and garnish with green onions and sesame seeds before serving.

Miso Black Bean Soup

Ingredients:

- 1 can black beans, rinsed and drained
- 4 cups vegetable broth
- 2 tbsp miso paste
- 1 onion, diced
- 2 cloves garlic, minced
- 1 tsp cumin
- Salt and pepper to taste

Instructions:

1. In a pot, sauté onion and garlic until softened.
2. Add black beans, vegetable broth, and cumin; bring to a boil.
3. Reduce heat, stir in miso paste, and season with salt and pepper. Simmer for 10-15 minutes before serving.

Miso Garlic Green Beans

Ingredients:

- 1 lb green beans, trimmed
- 2 tbsp miso paste
- 2 cloves garlic, minced
- 1 tbsp olive oil
- 1 tbsp sesame oil

Instructions:

1. Blanch green beans in boiling water for 3 minutes; drain and set aside.
2. In a skillet, heat olive oil and sauté garlic until fragrant.
3. Add green beans and miso paste; toss to coat. Drizzle with sesame oil before serving.

Miso Cauliflower Steaks

Ingredients:

- 1 head cauliflower, sliced into thick steaks
- 3 tbsp miso paste
- 2 tbsp olive oil
- 1 tbsp lemon juice
- Salt and pepper to taste

Instructions:

1. Preheat oven to 400°F (200°C).
2. In a bowl, mix miso paste, olive oil, and lemon juice.
3. Brush the mixture onto cauliflower steaks and season with salt and pepper.
4. Roast in the oven for 20-25 minutes until tender and golden.

Miso-Coconut Soup

Ingredients:

- 1 can coconut milk
- 4 cups vegetable broth
- 2 tbsp miso paste
- 1 cup mushrooms, sliced
- 1 cup bok choy, chopped
- 1 tbsp ginger, minced

Instructions:

1. In a pot, combine coconut milk and vegetable broth; bring to a simmer.
2. Stir in miso paste, mushrooms, bok choy, and ginger.
3. Cook for 10-15 minutes until vegetables are tender.

Miso Quinoa Salad

Ingredients:

- 1 cup quinoa, cooked
- 1/4 cup miso paste
- 2 tbsp olive oil
- 1 cup cherry tomatoes, halved
- 1 cucumber, diced
- Fresh herbs (e.g., parsley, cilantro)

Instructions:

1. In a bowl, whisk together miso paste and olive oil.
2. Combine cooked quinoa, cherry tomatoes, cucumber, and herbs in a large bowl.
3. Drizzle with the miso dressing and toss to combine before serving.

Miso Glazed Salmon

Ingredients:

- 4 salmon fillets
- 3 tbsp miso paste
- 2 tbsp honey
- 1 tbsp soy sauce
- Sesame seeds (for garnish)

Instructions:

1. Preheat oven to 375°F (190°C).
2. In a bowl, mix miso paste, honey, and soy sauce.
3. Brush the glaze over salmon fillets and place on a baking sheet.
4. Bake for 15-20 minutes until cooked through. Garnish with sesame seeds.

Miso Hummus

Ingredients:

- 1 can chickpeas, rinsed and drained
- 3 tbsp miso paste
- 2 tbsp tahini
- 2 tbsp lemon juice
- 2 cloves garlic, minced
- Olive oil (for drizzling)

Instructions:

1. In a food processor, combine chickpeas, miso paste, tahini, lemon juice, and garlic.
2. Blend until smooth, adding water if needed for consistency.
3. Serve drizzled with olive oil.

Miso Potatoes Au Gratin

Ingredients:

- 4 cups thinly sliced potatoes
- 1 cup heavy cream
- 1/4 cup miso paste
- 1 cup shredded cheese (e.g., Gruyère or cheddar)
- 2 cloves garlic, minced
- Salt and pepper to taste

Instructions:

1. Preheat the oven to 375°F (190°C).
2. In a bowl, whisk together heavy cream, miso paste, garlic, salt, and pepper.
3. Layer half of the sliced potatoes in a greased baking dish, then pour half of the cream mixture over them.
4. Repeat with the remaining potatoes and cream mixture, then top with shredded cheese.
5. Bake for 45-50 minutes until potatoes are tender and the top is golden.

Miso Cabbage Slaw

Ingredients:

- 4 cups shredded cabbage
- 1 carrot, grated
- 1/4 cup miso paste
- 2 tbsp apple cider vinegar
- 1 tbsp sesame oil
- 1 tbsp honey
- Green onions for garnish

Instructions:

1. In a bowl, whisk together miso paste, vinegar, sesame oil, and honey until smooth.
2. In a large mixing bowl, combine shredded cabbage and grated carrot.
3. Pour the miso dressing over the vegetables and toss to coat.
4. Garnish with sliced green onions before serving.

Miso and Maple Roasted Squash

Ingredients:

- 2 cups cubed butternut squash
- 2 tbsp miso paste
- 2 tbsp maple syrup
- 1 tbsp olive oil
- Salt and pepper to taste

Instructions:

1. Preheat the oven to 400°F (200°C).
2. In a bowl, mix miso paste, maple syrup, olive oil, salt, and pepper.
3. Toss the cubed squash in the miso mixture until evenly coated.
4. Spread on a baking sheet and roast for 25-30 minutes until tender and caramelized.

Miso Flatbread

Ingredients:

- 2 cups flour
- 1 tbsp miso paste
- 1/2 cup water
- 1 tbsp olive oil
- 1 tsp baking powder
- Salt to taste

Instructions:

1. In a bowl, mix flour, baking powder, and salt.
2. In a separate bowl, whisk together miso paste, water, and olive oil.
3. Combine the wet and dry ingredients, kneading until a dough forms.
4. Divide the dough into small balls and roll out into flatbreads.
5. Cook on a hot skillet for 2-3 minutes on each side until golden.

Miso Risotto

Ingredients:

- 1 cup Arborio rice
- 4 cups vegetable broth
- 1/4 cup miso paste
- 1 onion, finely chopped
- 2 cloves garlic, minced
- 1 cup peas
- 1/2 cup Parmesan cheese (optional)
- Olive oil for cooking

Instructions:

1. In a pot, heat olive oil and sauté onion and garlic until translucent.
2. Add Arborio rice and stir for 1-2 minutes.
3. Gradually add vegetable broth, one ladle at a time, stirring constantly until absorbed.
4. Once the rice is creamy and al dente, stir in miso paste, peas, and Parmesan cheese.

Miso Aioli

Ingredients:

- 1/2 cup mayonnaise
- 2 tbsp miso paste
- 1 tbsp lemon juice
- 1 clove garlic, minced
- Salt and pepper to taste

Instructions:

1. In a bowl, combine mayonnaise, miso paste, lemon juice, and garlic.
2. Mix until smooth and season with salt and pepper to taste.
3. Serve as a dip or spread.

Miso Stuffed Peppers

Ingredients:

- 4 bell peppers, halved and seeded
- 1 cup cooked quinoa
- 1/2 cup miso paste
- 1 cup diced vegetables (e.g., zucchini, carrots)
- 1 cup shredded cheese (optional)

Instructions:

1. Preheat the oven to 375°F (190°C).
2. In a bowl, mix cooked quinoa, miso paste, and diced vegetables.
3. Fill each bell pepper half with the quinoa mixture and top with cheese if desired.
4. Place in a baking dish and bake for 25-30 minutes until peppers are tender.

Miso Spinach Sauté

Ingredients:

- 4 cups fresh spinach
- 2 tbsp miso paste
- 2 cloves garlic, minced
- 1 tbsp sesame oil
- 1 tbsp soy sauce

Instructions:

1. In a skillet, heat sesame oil and sauté garlic until fragrant.
2. Add spinach and cook until wilted.
3. Stir in miso paste and soy sauce, mixing until evenly coated before serving.

Miso Noodle Salad

Ingredients:

- 8 oz soba noodles
- 1/4 cup miso paste
- 2 tbsp rice vinegar
- 1 tbsp sesame oil
- 1 cup shredded carrots
- 1 cup cucumber, thinly sliced
- 1/2 cup green onions, sliced
- Sesame seeds for garnish

Instructions:

1. Cook soba noodles according to package instructions, then rinse under cold water.
2. In a bowl, whisk together miso paste, rice vinegar, and sesame oil.
3. In a large bowl, combine cooked noodles, carrots, cucumber, and green onions.
4. Pour dressing over the salad and toss to combine.
5. Garnish with sesame seeds before serving.

Miso Gravy

Ingredients:

- 1/4 cup miso paste
- 2 cups vegetable broth
- 2 tbsp flour
- 2 tbsp olive oil
- 1 onion, finely chopped
- 2 cloves garlic, minced
- Pepper to taste

Instructions:

1. In a saucepan, heat olive oil and sauté onion and garlic until soft.
2. Whisk in flour and cook for 1 minute.
3. Gradually add vegetable broth, whisking to prevent lumps.
4. Stir in miso paste and bring to a simmer, cooking until thickened.
5. Season with pepper before serving.

Miso Eggplant Stir-Fry

Ingredients:

- 1 large eggplant, cubed
- 2 tbsp miso paste
- 2 tbsp soy sauce
- 1 tbsp sesame oil
- 1 bell pepper, sliced
- 2 cloves garlic, minced
- 1 inch ginger, grated

Instructions:

1. In a bowl, mix miso paste, soy sauce, and sesame oil.
2. Heat a pan over medium heat and add eggplant, cooking until tender.
3. Add bell pepper, garlic, and ginger, cooking for an additional 3-4 minutes.
4. Pour the miso mixture over the vegetables and toss to coat, cooking for another 2 minutes.

Miso and Lemon Grilled Chicken

Ingredients:

- 4 chicken breasts
- 1/4 cup miso paste
- Juice of 1 lemon
- 2 tbsp olive oil
- 2 cloves garlic, minced
- Salt and pepper to taste

Instructions:

1. In a bowl, mix miso paste, lemon juice, olive oil, garlic, salt, and pepper.
2. Coat the chicken breasts with the marinade and let sit for at least 30 minutes.
3. Preheat the grill and cook chicken for 6-7 minutes on each side, until cooked through.

Miso Chilled Noodle Bowl

Ingredients:

- 8 oz udon noodles
- 1/4 cup miso paste
- 2 tbsp soy sauce
- 1 tbsp sesame oil
- 1 cup shredded vegetables (e.g., carrots, cucumbers)
- Fresh herbs for garnish

Instructions:

1. Cook udon noodles according to package instructions, then rinse under cold water.
2. In a bowl, whisk together miso paste, soy sauce, and sesame oil.
3. In a large bowl, combine cooled noodles and shredded vegetables.
4. Pour dressing over the noodles and toss to combine.
5. Garnish with fresh herbs before serving.

Miso Braised Short Ribs

Ingredients:

- 2 lbs short ribs
- 1/4 cup miso paste
- 2 cups beef broth
- 1/4 cup soy sauce
- 2 tbsp honey
- 2 cloves garlic, minced

Instructions:

1. Preheat oven to 300°F (150°C).
2. In a bowl, mix miso paste, beef broth, soy sauce, honey, and garlic.
3. Place short ribs in a baking dish and pour the miso mixture over them.
4. Cover with foil and braise in the oven for 3 hours until tender.

Miso Potato Salad

Ingredients:

- 4 cups diced potatoes
- 1/4 cup miso paste
- 1/4 cup mayonnaise
- 2 tbsp apple cider vinegar
- 1/4 cup chopped green onions
- Salt and pepper to taste

Instructions:

1. Boil potatoes until tender, then drain and cool.
2. In a bowl, mix miso paste, mayonnaise, vinegar, salt, and pepper.
3. Add cooled potatoes and green onions, mixing gently to combine.

Miso Glazed Tofu

Ingredients:

- 14 oz firm tofu, cubed
- 1/4 cup miso paste
- 2 tbsp soy sauce
- 1 tbsp maple syrup
- 1 tbsp sesame oil

Instructions:

1. In a bowl, mix miso paste, soy sauce, maple syrup, and sesame oil.
2. Toss cubed tofu in the marinade and let sit for at least 30 minutes.
3. Preheat oven to 400°F (200°C) and bake tofu for 25-30 minutes, turning halfway through, until golden and caramelized.

Miso Dipping Sauce for Veggies

Ingredients:

- 1/4 cup miso paste
- 2 tbsp sesame oil
- 1 tbsp rice vinegar
- 1 tbsp honey
- 1-2 tbsp water (to thin)

Instructions:

1. In a bowl, whisk together miso paste, sesame oil, rice vinegar, and honey.
2. Add water gradually until the desired consistency is reached.
3. Serve with assorted fresh vegetables for dipping.

Miso Chive Butter

Ingredients:

- 1/2 cup unsalted butter, softened
- 2 tbsp miso paste
- 1/4 cup fresh chives, chopped

Instructions:

1. In a bowl, mix softened butter with miso paste until well combined.
2. Stir in chopped chives.
3. Transfer to parchment paper, roll into a log, and refrigerate until firm.

Miso Sweet Potato Soup

Ingredients:

- 2 large sweet potatoes, peeled and cubed
- 1 onion, chopped
- 3 cups vegetable broth
- 1/4 cup miso paste
- 1 tbsp olive oil
- Salt and pepper to taste

Instructions:

1. In a pot, heat olive oil and sauté onion until soft.
2. Add sweet potatoes and vegetable broth; bring to a boil.
3. Reduce heat and simmer until sweet potatoes are tender.
4. Stir in miso paste and blend until smooth. Season with salt and pepper.

Miso Potato Wedges

Ingredients:

- 4 medium potatoes, cut into wedges
- 1/4 cup miso paste
- 2 tbsp olive oil
- 1 tbsp sesame seeds
- Salt and pepper to taste

Instructions:

1. Preheat oven to 425°F (220°C).
2. In a bowl, mix miso paste, olive oil, sesame seeds, salt, and pepper.
3. Toss potato wedges in the mixture until well coated.
4. Spread on a baking sheet and roast for 25-30 minutes until golden and crispy.

Miso Vegetable Tempura

Ingredients:

- Assorted vegetables (e.g., bell peppers, zucchini, sweet potato)
- 1/4 cup miso paste
- 1/2 cup water
- 1 cup tempura flour
- Oil for frying

Instructions:

1. Heat oil in a deep pan for frying.
2. In a bowl, mix miso paste with water, then gradually add tempura flour until smooth.
3. Dip vegetable pieces in batter and fry until golden and crispy.
4. Drain on paper towels before serving.

Miso Peach Glaze

Ingredients:

- 1/4 cup miso paste
- 1/4 cup peach preserves
- 1 tbsp rice vinegar
- 1 tbsp soy sauce

Instructions:

1. In a saucepan, combine miso paste, peach preserves, rice vinegar, and soy sauce.
2. Heat over medium heat, stirring until smooth and well blended.
3. Use as a glaze for grilled meats or vegetables.

Miso Stuffed Mushrooms

Ingredients:

- 12 large mushrooms, stems removed
- 1/4 cup miso paste
- 1/2 cup breadcrumbs
- 1/4 cup grated Parmesan cheese
- 2 tbsp olive oil

Instructions:

1. Preheat oven to 375°F (190°C).
2. In a bowl, mix miso paste, breadcrumbs, Parmesan cheese, and olive oil.
3. Stuff each mushroom cap with the mixture.
4. Bake for 20 minutes until mushrooms are tender and topping is golden.

Miso Roasted Chickpeas

Ingredients:

- 1 can (15 oz) chickpeas, drained and rinsed
- 2 tbsp miso paste
- 1 tbsp olive oil
- 1 tsp garlic powder
- Salt to taste

Instructions:

1. Preheat oven to 400°F (200°C).
2. In a bowl, mix chickpeas with miso paste, olive oil, garlic powder, and salt.
3. Spread chickpeas on a baking sheet and roast for 25-30 minutes until crispy.

Miso Tomato Sauce

Ingredients:

- 1 can (28 oz) crushed tomatoes
- 1/4 cup miso paste
- 1 tbsp olive oil
- 2 cloves garlic, minced
- 1 tsp dried oregano
- 1 tsp sugar (optional)
- Salt and pepper to taste

Instructions:

1. In a saucepan, heat olive oil over medium heat and sauté minced garlic until fragrant.
2. Add crushed tomatoes and miso paste, stirring until the miso is dissolved.
3. Stir in oregano and sugar if using, and let simmer for 15-20 minutes.
4. Season with salt and pepper before serving over pasta or as a base for other dishes.

Miso and Seaweed Salad

Ingredients:

- 1 cup dried seaweed (wakame or similar)
- 1 tbsp miso paste
- 2 tbsp rice vinegar
- 1 tbsp sesame oil
- 1 tbsp soy sauce
- 1 tsp sugar
- 1/4 cup green onions, chopped
- Sesame seeds for garnish

Instructions:

1. Rehydrate dried seaweed in warm water for about 10 minutes, then drain and squeeze out excess water.
2. In a bowl, whisk together miso paste, rice vinegar, sesame oil, soy sauce, and sugar until smooth.
3. Add the rehydrated seaweed and chopped green onions to the dressing, tossing to combine.
4. Garnish with sesame seeds before serving.

www.ingramcontent.com/pod-product-compliance
Lightning Source LLC
LaVergne TN
LVHW081334060526
838201LV00055B/2637